Petrichor

MOHAMMED ABRAR AHMED
(@thficklepoet)

First published by Mohammed Abrar Ahmed 2022

Copyright © 2022 by Mohammed Abrar Ahmed

All rights reserved. No part of this publication may be reproduced, stored, or transmitted in any form or by any means, electronic, mechanical, photocopying, recording, scanning, or otherwise without written permission from the publisher. It is illegal to copy this book, post it to a website or distribute it by any other means without permission.

First edition

ISBN: 978-0-9979824-3-5

Email: contact@mohdabrar.com

*To the friends old who stuck by me,
and new ones who saved me without realizing.
To Hamza, I miss you. To the love that left,
and to the love that hasn't arrived yet.*

Contents

Foreword ix

Thunderstorm
    An Autopsy of My Suicide. 2
    Remnants 4
    Earlier 6
    I Don't Want to Go Home Sometimes. 7
    Emptiness 9
    A Letter to My Son 10
    Aftermath 13
    Sodden Memories 14
    Tangled 15
    Uncertainty 16
    Pain's Consideration 17
    Last Words 18
    Leaving Mementos 19

Rain
    I was a Love Poet Once 22
    Dear Me 24
    Under 25 Words 26
    Sound of Silence 27
    Life Didn't Go as Planned 29
    Always on My Mind 31
    For the Lack of It. 33
    Trading Battle Scars. 34
    A Dance with Death 35
    Love or Lesson. 36

Thunderstorms 37
Hanging 38
Love Knocking 39
Again. 40
When You Lose Me 41
It Should Not Be Named. 42
Sucker Punched. 43
Moments. 44
Happy. 45
Broken 1 46
Broken 2 47
Broken 3 48
Life Support 49
The Reason I Write 50
Death 52
Done. 53
Whispers. 54
Conversations that Kill You. 55
False Goodbyes 56
Sadness 57

Calm

Her 60
What Else is Left? 61
Daylight 62
Perfection 64
Days Like These (A Song) 65
A Conversation with Her. 66
A Conversation I Will Never Have with Her 67
A Conversation I Want to have with Her. 69
Cold Water 70
Always on My Mind 72
September Love. 74
Falling. 75

Trip & Fall	76
Finding Her	77
Not Going to Happen	78
A Broken Mind	79
Misfits	80
The Traveller	82
Improvised	83
Warm You Up	84
Angels	85
Black & White	86
See	87
Surviving You	88
Tale of the Red Scarf	89
Knowing	90
November	91
Listen	92
What She Said	93
Maybe – The Beginning	94
Maybe Part – 1	95
Maybe Part – 2	96
Maybe Part – 3	97
Maybe – The Final Chapter	99
Closing Arguments	100
When Night Comes On	101
Silence	102
2 AM	103
Strings	104
Love	105
The Final Dialogue	106
Thirty-Five	107
Petrichor	110
About the Author	112

Foreword

After reading a few pages of this book, I texted Abrar to say it's not an easy read. If I were to define it, it's a book that brings back the memories you buried long ago. It makes you walk in the streets where your last goodbyes live. This book will take you to the places you felt almost comfortable in, but you never belonged. The words spread on these pages will pierce your heart and bring out the people who were home, but it's been long since you have visited them. And in the midst of it all, Abrar makes you walk to the mirror in your house and look at your reflection. He holds your hand and tells you that you are a survivor; you need to let the pain go, you are also human, a blend of flaws and perfection. Finally, you will find yourself lying in the grass and inhaling the petrichor.

Huma Adnan, author of Once the Birds Fly

Thunderstorm

An Autopsy of My Suicide

He is here — there are no wounds, no blood, just a corpse. Mine. This empty shell of a body with dead eyes. Let me take you back to where it began.

Toronto, 23rd November 2020 — A cold winter evening, the kind of cold that cuts through the bone. 5:37 PM, an empty airport. A forced exit. Life as he knew stood still. He hugged his three-year-old son before settling him back in the car seat and left. That was the last time he held his son. Maybe he was already dead at this point.

Maybe I need to take you back a little further...

10th October 2020 — A frosty fall. A house full of people, a loneliness that could not be shared. A married couple, a broken rail, creaking floorboards, and a deafening silence only masked by the laughter of a child. Working his ass off every day only to be told, "Your efforts are appreciated, but we've got it covered." Words that made him stop in his tracks and freeze the marrow in his bones.

Or I think I know when he died...

17th September 2020 — The beginning of autumn and the start of his end. Days blending into nights, time stood still. Love walked out of the door, never to return. Two bodies in a house that never crossed paths. Meals eaten separately; tears shed alone. The only soul who doesn't understand the silence is a three-year-old child. The kid is happy when he sees him; runs into his arms when he returns from work. So, he returns every evening. For that laugh which echoes in a rather quiet house.

Left alone with his thoughts at night, when the crickets come out to sing. He came down the flight of stairs and held a kitchen knife to his wrist; the cold metal met his skin. Tears streaming down his face, quenching the thirst of an unkept promise. A smile comes to his mind. And so, he lived, with no will to go on.

The next morning, he lost his voice. No words were uttered. His shoulders drooped when he walked, dragging his feet on the ground like he was carrying the weight of the world. His smile buried in the backyard, under the stars. He died last night.

No blood was spilled, no scars visible. A moving corpse is what remains. No warmth, just a cold body. Unloved…

Remnants

I rise every morning, not from my grave, but from my bed where I disappear every night, after a day filled with fake laughter, broken promises, and ultimatums.

I rise because I cannot drown or bury myself under the very earth I walk on. I collect mementos and make up stories of how we went on a walk and found that flower, growing against all odds, resisting nature in the middle of winter amidst the snow. It eventually will wither away like every other living thing on this planet.

I remember saying to her once that I'd love her no matter what. And I did. It took every mitochondrion in my body to survive her and stand back on my own two feet. I remember how the words pierced my soul every time we spoke. I kept silent but you thought of it as a weakness and tried your best to put me down and you succeeded too. Almost…

I roam with the remnants of your piercing words, still etched into my bones, your silence when I was disrespected by your respected family. When I was asked to leave the home, I worked for every day. Memories of playing with my son, which you said were just for show. I remember waking up every day and wanting to die. I wondered how someone who cared, doesn't care anymore. These remnants remind me that I no longer have the skin that has been touched by you. That I am no longer the person I used to be. That I know what I am worth now and what you put me through was torture.

I was wrong to endure it, I did any way. Maybe I am at fault. Maybe, I shouldn't have taken so long to realise I am no longer welcome into the home that I thought was ours. Thank you for reminding me that it never was.

I can't wait to see what I make out of these hollowed bones, damaged lungs, and a sewed-up heart. You left me in ruins, and I will make a castle out of these bones…

Earlier

I think about the time, us,
from before and I do not
really remember most of it.
We were one day and
then we were not anymore.
You and I were a contradiction
but we managed
to be together
against all odds
only to live as strangers
under one roof.

Sometimes when I am sitting
alone in my room,
facing a taunting cursor on my
screen, I remember about the
times we spent together.
How it was love and nothing else.
And in the end, there was just nothing.
How you used to wake me up
With your kisses and I started waking
up alone, with you in the other room.
I think about it, every now and then
And I tell myself, it must all have been a
dream, whatever that was — earlier.

I Don't Want to Go Home Sometimes

I don't want to go home sometimes. I walk around, trying to delay the journey of reaching an empty room. I hold myself back from opening the door as much as possible. I move slowly with no motivation to head towards the empty room that I call home now. There's no one waiting for me at home. So, I walk taking the longer routes just to delay the destination. But eventually I need to rest someplace, somewhere.

I've walked to work in winters, a heavy jacket on my shoulders. I walk through the snow, leaving my shoe prints, that lead me back home in the evening because no one wants to take a used trail in the snow. When it snows, nobody thinks they'd walk somewhere that day.

I've walked when it's hot outside, when the sun is about to set but just wants to burn the earth a little more before it finally says it's done for the day. I wish it would burn me alive sometimes. I wish I didn't have to face an empty bed to come to the realization that whatever I do this void isn't going to be filled. No matter how long I stay out, things are not going to get better.

Eventually they will, that's what people tell me...

I walk home in the evening, and I walk away from home in the middle of the night when no one is looking. I hope the night would just swallow me alive, but that doesn't happen either. Just yesterday someone asked me, "Aren't you afraid of what is in the dark?" And I replied, "I am not, shouldn't whatever's in the dark be afraid of me who's walking in the middle of the night knowing there could be something in the dark?" How fucked up it must be for someone who is surrounded by people all day only to be alone at night. I am not saying I don't like to be alone. I like my company, I have been alone, battling my demons for a long time now. That empty home reminds me how lonely I have gotten over time. It snaps me back to the painful reality that I don't like it here anymore. I don't know how I am going to survive this, but I know for sure, if I make it to tomorrow and someone asks me how am I doing? My answer's going to be "Good!" with a forced smile and a sparkle in my eyes like I mean it. I have gotten good at hiding my emotions now.

I survived last night; I looked into the mirror and convinced the person in it to live one more day in the hopes that something good might happen. I got asked this morning how I was doing — and just as every day, I smiled and said, "Good, thank you. And you?" I don't know for how long I can keep this ruse up, but it's getting difficult again.

Emptiness

Hey, if you're reading this, I'm not doing good. I am at the edge, over and over again. Almost every night. I am flipping through pages that I have written over and over, trying to make sense of it but everything is nonsense. Nothing is making sense anymore. It's empty. Everything is empty…

It's 12:00 AM and I am outside right now. I don't see a single soul. I am sitting on a bench, holding a cigarette, too scared to put it in between my lips. This is my fourth. I just keep lighting them. It's unusually windy tonight. The wind finishes them off before I can even bring them to my lips.

It hurts. I don't know about this pain. It's too much to bear but at the same time it's been with me all my life. I don't know what I am doing with it and I don't even know what I should be doing with it. I have no idea what to do. So, I sit here in the middle of nowhere, 12:00 AM, thinking of all the possible things that I can do wrong. There isn't anything else to do tomorrow anyway, right? So, I don't have to wake up tomorrow. Should I? I don't know I haven't thought that far yet. I don't know if I should. It hurts. I used to have all the answers but I just… don't anymore. I don't even know the questions to ask. I don't have the words. I don't have anything anymore…

A Letter to My Son

Dear Hamza, As-salamu alaykum (May peace be upon you). I know you are aware how to reply to this, as you've been taught to do so. I don't know when or if you'll ever get to read this, but I wanted to let you know —

You will be turning five
in six months and I am sorry,
that I am not with you.
Trust me when I say
it was not my decision
to be away from you.
And I beat myself up every day
for not being with you.
We talk almost everyday
on video calls, but that
doesn't really help you,
at an age when I need
to be present physically,
we're dealing with emotions
electronically.
You seem to have the same
temper that I do.
I was hoping you didn't,
but I was sure, that I could
help you guide it from early
on, but seems like life had
some other plans.

I hope someone teaches you
to control the anger that
bursts inside of you,
don't let the frustration get
the best of you, the reeling
damage of one episode of
anger can send you in a
downward spiral. Trust me,
I've been there. There was
no one to guide me through
it, but if you read this, sit down.
Count to ten, smile, like I
taught you, breathe,
let go of what stops you.
I know it's difficult to not
react, but don't. Just until you
know you have a lid on it.
Don't let bullies bully you,
this is where you take the
lid off. Be soft when you
speak, stand up when your
elders walk in, leave the room
if you're not part of the
conversation. I know you're
too young to be told all this,
but I am just writing this down,
in case I never get a chance to
tell you in person. If you
ever feel like crying, do that,
don't bottle it up. And don't
let anyone tell you, that
boys don't cry. I do.
It helps you to move on,
learn to laugh when you're

in pain. It confuses people.
Cry when you're happy to
mess with their heads.
Always be humble.

Love fiercely and
keep your promises.
Open doors for the ladies,
even when they mistake it
for flirting, be chivalrous.
We're a dying breed.
Think with your heart,
but decide from your mind.
If something doesn't feel
good, it probably isn't.
Take risks in life, travel
every opportunity you get.
Make memories, stay true
to your faith.

Call me often, try to forgive me,
for not being present, I am sorry.
I missed your golden years,
and I don't know how much more
I will miss but I will always be a
phone call away. Remember me
at every milestone.

And most importantly, never leave
your mother alone. I will see you soon…

Aftermath

Forgotten,
rotting away,
droopy eyes,
in the middle
of the desert.
Slowly fading
from existence,
roaming endlessly,
with no direction.
This soulless body,
now hears no heeds,
It travels wherever
the wind blows.
Baggy eyes,
fake smiles,
loud laughter,
cloudy nights,
the aftermath
of a destruction,
a hurricane, like
no other.

Here he starts,
after a brief stop…

Sodden Memories

A heavy heart,
a mind soaked
with traces of
your memories,
bringing me back
to an empty bed,
drowning me in
a void, a vacuum,
where my screams
go unheard and
every hurtful word
ever uttered, etched
on the walls of this
skull, come to life
to haunt me,
the monster in me
wants to fight back
but the weight of these
sodden memories,
keep me still…

Afraid, but very still…

Tangled

Hands and legs cuffed to the bed,
a rainstorm outside,
thunder, then lightning follows,
sweet kisses of forever,
until the mind wakes,
from the imagination that it created.

I am tangled in your memories
of sweet disposition
a dangerous mind game,
that will be the end of me…

Uncertainty

Every single thought that connects to another could be unrealistic. Sometimes deemed stupid or idiotic, a nuisance to self. The uncertainty of not knowing what lies next for me gives me anxiety, irrevocable pain and impiety. What will I lose next, what will I gain? Is it pain, fame, love, or another mundane name?

Unrecognizable, laughter so magical, it's tragical, eyes say something and face shows nothing. The body fighting to give in, give up every night. I go to bed uncertain if this will be my last night. I revise my will, every other night, like clockwork. Magical things come to life in my mind and keep me awake at night. As if the mind wants to keep a track of what goes on during the night, the shadows that leave me, the monsters that hug me, the never-ending pillow fights, all a delight to imagine for a mind too alone to be called lonely, too loving to be closed, too hurt to be loved again.

The uncertainty of what lies tomorrow does not let me live in peace today and if I am to die tonight, all I wish for is to live another day…

Pain's Consideration

It was in the absence of love,
that I felt numbing pain.
And when love knocked
on this heart again,
pain whispered,
I'll stay just until you're sure,
if you really want me to leave...

Last Words

Nothing was ever said
all the love and promises
were forgotten.

In the end all I got was
a "fuck you" and
a ride to the airport…

My last words,
"Treat the next one kindly."

Leaving Mementos

My heart is pacing
for I haven't experienced
this kind of adrenaline
as I did today, since you left...

You want to know
what I did?
I thought of every
demeaning word
you ever uttered
to me and ran
leaving its pieces
all over this town

You don't weigh
me down anymore...

Rain

I was a Love Poet Once

To me love was a magical emotion, a commotion to stop in one's step when our eyes met; how beautiful those lips look, I wish they could be felt.

If only I could find myself again, maybe I could explain what this feeling is and how it felt when I experienced her touch but never really touched her. How she puts a leash on my imagination and her smile has that irresistible fascination. How sometimes she says things that makes no sense and sometimes, the conversations turn so deep that it pains.

I was a love poet once. I don't write about love anymore but if I were to write about love one more time, I would tell you about how I imagine myself, alone, on a beach at night, the sound of the sea, crashing every time on the shore. Falling so hard that it leaves a mark. I sit there, looking at the vast nothingness, so empty, it fills the universe. I hear her footsteps approaching with caution, as she plans to close my eyes with her hands and wants me to guess who it is. Little does she know that her fragrance had already made her presence felt. So close yet so distant. I could touch her if I want to, but I don't. She sits beside me on a cold November night, looking into the same void as I do and says, "It's so full." That's the balance life looks for. If I were to write about love again, I would say this would be it. She would be it. A mole near her eye, the way she adjusts her hair every few minutes because they refuse to stay in one place. The way she innocently cracks a joke and we both laugh. A beach where we both are, right in this moment but not together because being in love doesn't guarantee togetherness, of course. The reality of accepting an unrequited love always stings but this time, I am going to float in it.

Every single time, I let love consume me from inside and it left scars on me that I still cannot get rid of. If I were to write about love once again, this would have to be it. To let it exist in its own path and not to force anything. I get to see her from a distance and appreciate the beauty that she is but never cross the line. Spend as much time I possibly can and understand that somethings in life are meant to cross your path and you need to let them go, they're on their journey. And if, by luck, as love always needs a fucking lot of it, she feels the same and the line is crossed and the paths are merged, the possibilities are endless.

I was a love a poet once and I can't seem to write about love's pain anymore, about how every scar love has ever left on this heart makes my heartbeat faster. How every action, I take has been thought out multiple times as to not come across as too clingy for someone; how it all feels worthless sometimes and not having it at the same time makes me feel worthless… If I were to write about love once again, I wouldn't. I would just want to have the courage to tell her…

Dear Me

How have you been?
It's been a while since we had a chat.
I don't sit in front of the mirror anymore,
I still hide behind my smile though.

To be honest I've missed you.
our late-night talks,
bottles of coke, do you remember
how much we used to drink
that it almost left us broke.

I left you behind when I left,
it was a new chapter,
but I must confess,
I've missed you…

Dear Me, I am sorry,
for handling you the way I did,
for leaving you with scars
that may take a lifelong to heal,
I thought it was the real deal.
I am back again in the shadows,
trying to find my way across
the cosmos, I am bruised,
broken, hanging by a thread,
like almost open.
I am sorry, for giving others priority over you,
I am sorry, for falling in love so recklessly every time,

I am sorry, I may be about to do it again.
I am sorry, for all the hurt I caused,
I am sorry, for laughing when I knew we were hurting,
I am sorry, that I don't open to people much,
and I am sorry that I've sometimes shared a lot.
I am sorry, for being a closed book for so long
that people thought you were an asshole.
I am sorry, dear me, for killing your dreams,
for driving headfirst into a light pole, wanting
to end the suffering only to add to it.
Dear Me, I am tired. The air has become heavy
and my lungs can't hold it in any longer…

With every breath I take, I feel everything is crumbling down on me, around me, so fast that I can't even say a word before it hits me. Buried deep, a wish to live a life so carefree but what I have is something entirely empty.

I am sorry, I am still not what I should be, but I've been told, I am enough…

Under 25 Words

On the precipice
of letting go,
I roam endlessly,
find my way to a cliff,
I had decided
to jump from.

I don't.

Sound of Silence

A home,
clatter of utensils.
Sound of water
gushing through the tap.
Phones vibrating,
children playing.

A hotel room,
elevator bell dings
every few minutes,
footsteps outside,
the wind swishing,
sometimes howling,
and sometimes whistling,
trying to get my
attention.

A sidewalk
full of people,
speaking a language
I don't understand,
cars honking,
scribble of pen
on paper, restaurants
orders being taken.

Everything,
all at once,

hits you like a
punch in the throat,
you don't respond.
You let it consume you.

Midnight,
everything is empty,
a home, no one talks.

A hotel room,
footsteps still heard
outside, people making
love, moans from
adjacent rooms.
Wind still howling,
whistling.

I hear everything
amidst the sound of
silence, except my
heart beating like it
used to, to the sound
of your name.

It responds to another
now…

Life Didn't Go as Planned

It was never supposed to, I am told. Life is complex. You don't know the next move it's going to make until you've been dealt the cards.

You plan something and life always has a way to screw it up. Years of hard work and pain you put into something can be taken away in an instant. Love that you thought will never leave you, will walk out the door so fast, you'll still be looking for words to respond. Or you'll keep looking for answers long after they've left. There aren't any. Let go of what has already left. Keep the door open. Let something new walk in. Let life deal with people who left you out, the same way you let life put you down. Every turn is an opportunity. Cherish it! Make new friends, love again and live to the fullest. Light those cigars, finish that book and smile often.

Everyone's fighting their demons, be an angel. Be kind, more often than not. Listen to what people have to say. Understand the consequences. Remember you'll fall in love again and you might have to let him/her go. Let them go. Let them know as well, you never know who will decide to stay. Don't plan ahead. Live by the day. Have goals and work on them. Whether you're twenty-five, thirty-five or fifty. Life can change your circumstances any moment. Be humble about it, always be ready. See everything as a challenge. Maybe life put you in position you are now in to make you grow. Hit rock bottom with grace. Cry, but be strong. Let it all go.

You're not guaranteed anything, if it comes your way, cherish it. If it leaves, understand. People, jobs and their place in your life is temporary. We make friends for life. Family is important, but they can drain you sometimes. Find your passion, maybe that's what you're meant to find when you lost that job, or when the person you loved left you. You might not have hit rock-bottom yet. Maybe you got to go lower than you've already fell to find that elevator to take you up. But always remember it might break midway and you might have to take the stairs. Take the damn fucking stairs…

Always remember, not everything you plan will come to fruition. You can either adjust or sit in denial about what happened. It took me a long time to understand this, I know it's going to be difficult in the beginning when everything you touch breaks. Every opportunity leaves you on the side-lines, then the ebb and flow of time gives you a chance to prove yourself again and you do and keep doing it, until you're on the top again.

The view is good, enjoy while it lasts, it can last a lifetime, or it can bring you down anytime. Be humble about it.

For life, is a game of snakes and ladders, and sometimes, you have to grab the snake by the tail to get bitten to get to where you want to be…

Always on My Mind

Time and time again
I hear myself scream
Don't let me go
Don't let me go
I wake up from a dream
The curves of your body
I want to feel
The love I have for you is real
I want to touch you
Hold you and kiss you
I'm in no way
Trying to fix you
I like you this way
Broken and confused
Every time I read you
I am amused
Your hand on my chest
And mine on your breast
Heartbeat synchronised
And both undressed
I place my kisses
On your tender flesh
I bite you a little
And then caress
I've given myself to you
And I have you in my arms
My life's in your hands

As my throat is in your palms
I tickle your ears
with my tongue a little
I sing you a song
Tell you I'm fickle
You bite my neck
Then tease me a little
You push me to the bed
The rest is not a riddle…

For the Lack of It

Everyday, there are events that repeat, in the same order as the previous day. I travel the same route everyday, and I see an old man entering the cemetery with flowers for his wife's grave.

I see a guy holding the hand of his girlfriend on a walk.

I see a lady watering the plants at the same time everyday, waving at me as I pass by, as if she was waiting for me.

I see an old man with his grandson at the park, who is coming down the slide.

I see a couple leave for work together.

I see them everyday, lonely in the midst of their loved ones, unnoticed, just waiting to live it out and be done with. They don't smile. They just are. For a reason or may be for the lack of it...

Trading Battle Scars

I am trading my battle scars for sacred nights under the stars — this shell of a body aches and aches, but I ignore every cell of my being screaming for me to stop. I look at the wounds on my hands, the scabs making a perfect map, a way back to you as if the first time wasn't enough.

This heart almost gave up, gave in, but doesn't quit to beat. I am trading my scars for now because the memories attached with these come at a cost which I am no longer willing to pay. I remember every single time I waited for you to show up, ultimatums did. I am learning to live without you, without a promise of tomorrow, protected under the moon and its sacred bond with the night that lights my path in your absence.

The stars shine brighter than they ever did before. Just like your eyes when you smiled, laughed or giggled. Everything's got to go, these memories of you, these scars, the lost paths and you.

I am trading everything to finally sleep, under open skies with stars as my blanket. Finally, I come undone...

A Dance with Death

It's been a while since I talked to myself. I have silenced the voices inside my head, whispering, nudging me to end it all.

I stopped listening. I stopped answering the call and kept moving on. Last night, she called again, telling me how sorry she was for messing it all up. That she won't let it happen again. That this time when I come close, she'll hold me closer than ever before.

A loving hug, making me suffocate and appreciate each breath I ever took. She looked me in the eye and held on hoping I'd go over the cliff with her, just like last time. I kissed her, then stepped back, leaving her standing on the edge. We shook hands and agreed we'll meet again soon, maybe when I've lived a little.

And just as I started to walk away, she pulled me down with her. My death, woke me up again...

Love or Lesson

I'm starting to wonder again,
if it's love that's knocking my door,
or just another lesson...

Thunderstorms

Thunderstorms in the desert,
Followed by rain to quench my thirst,
You, a calm before the storm...

Hanging

Here I am once again,
Hanging by a thread to not let go.
To not fall in love...

Love Knocking

It hurts to come
To the realization
That after everything
I've been through
I could still fall in love
With someone
Who will never
Love me back...

Again

Love is like an unbearable
weight on one's chest.
You think the weight lifts
when you acknowledge
that you're in love
and let the other person
know how you feel...

But what happens when you can't?
How heavy does this
feeling need to get
before your eyes get heavy,
but start losing sleep
and eventually yourself?
How will you pull yourself
back from the pit a second time?
How could someone
fall in the pit a second time?

Why the fuck does this keep happening to me?

When You Lose Me

She'll never realise
what she has lost.
And if she ever does,
she'd have already lost...

The wounds would
have already filled,
the scars will tell
the story of an impasse.
Cold winter breaths,
met the burning sun.
Short laps that were run,
were never fun.
Darkness and light,
two sides of a fight.
What you follow
is what you'll get,
in the end,
let there be no regrets.

It Should Not Be Named

I am starting to feel that rush again, the adrenaline that drives you to not think of any consequences. The carelessness that makes you just dive into things that may not be meant for you...

I've been at these crossroads before and I've been at the depths of this pit, it's going to get worse before it gets better. Whatever this is, it's different every time and it only goes by one name...

And once you call it by its name, you must accept that you're already in deep and the worse has begun...

Sucker Punched

What I hate about falling in love with someone is you never get to decide if you want to.

You just do and when the realization creeps in, you're already too fucking deep. And knowing well that things will never work out, not in your favor, but in love's. So that takes away that little faith you keep for love that it'll eventually find you.

Moments

I lie here
in this dark room,
alone.
And all I hear
is her laughter.
I realise now,
that it's going to be
a long and hard
battle to forget her.

Happy

I used to walk around with a frown on my face, but of late I can't help but smile and be happy. I sometimes feel I am at a good place, spiritually, getting things done that need to be done.

But nothing lasts for ever. Happiness or sorrow, or the joy in your marrow. Everything comes to an end, eventually. Either by people who cannot stand to watch you happy or by your own doing.

I was naïve to think it would be different this time, that no one can sabotage what it is and this feeling will remain for a while. I had made up my mind, that it would eventually collapse, whatever it was and I was right. Things got out of hand and everything tumbled down overnight.

Knowing myself and my track record, I had always seen this coming and I know it shouldn't be hurting this much, but it fucking does and I have no idea why. It's like I know I am going to punch myself in the windpipe and it will hurt and I am ready for the pain, but doing so and bearing the pain, are two different things.

Another lesson learnt, to never allow yourself to be happy. Because someone is always lurking around to fucking take it away.

Broken 1

They were singing songs,
he had just learnt.
They were going to be parents.
Everything has its limits.

The drunken driver was way past his…

Broken 2

She called him inside,
he refused in a fit of rage.
She said, "You're just like your father."

He came in instantly and hugged her.

"Mom, I'm never going to walk out on you," he said.

He was five and growing up quickly.

Broken 3

"Do you ever think of the loss we endured?"

she asked him, while he was playing a video game.

"Why do you think I always play his favourite game?"

he asked.

They broke into tears...

Life Support

Have you ever been to a hospital? There are different procedures for different diagnoses. There are patients coding for whom they bring in the crash cart to revive them and then there are people who come in with hiccups and end up dead.

Then there are those who are fighting to live. They undergo surgery after surgery until they cannot anymore and understand that it's time, they stop the fight. People on life support tend to make doctors happy when they fight through and come out of it because they are breathing on their own now. They are safe.

Then there are those who fight and lose. They are comatose, brain dead or just lost the will to wake up and they hurt the most. For them, life is a joy, which they are fighting to attain.

For some time now, I have been feeling plugged in to something or someone who does not even have any clue about my existence. I unintentionally made them my life support and I know this connection needs to be severed at some point in life, as this will only complicate things for me. We are not doctors, we are merely incapable people who cannot make the decision whether to let go or hold on. We make people our life support and threaten to take ourselves off life support if they let go of us.

Love demands to be the life support; it will kill you if you let go of it from your hearts.

The Reason I Write

I write to tell the things that I want to talk about but have no one to talk to. I've been hurt, ridiculed, laughed at and thrown away far too many times for the way I think, talk or behave, just about anything. And I believe a voice in me dies every time something like that happens and this is how I let my steam out.

I don't care if my words matter or they don't, if they are read and felt or not, if they believe in me or don't, I don't write for fame or money. All I care about are the thoughts that wake me up at 2 a.m. in the morning are the same that someone else is going through and I just want to connect with someone, to know that I am not the only one.

I write because I loved, I fell in deeper than I should have and the only way I could say all the things to her is through poetry. If she is never going to love me back, at least she could read what I had to say to her and not hate me.

And the most important reason of all, I've been told, is when you can create something out of nothing, anything, you fucking do it. When you can paint a picture with words, it's in you to do it.

And that's why I write. Because I want to share. Share a story, a day in my life, with the right mix of fiction and reality. And none of these is a good enough reason that I think is required to write. All I have is a heart that loves, a mind that's high without drugs or alcohol or cigarettes I have a story and I sometimes can't differentiate the reality from imagination. So, I write.

Death

It is inevitable, death.
The sheer rush of it
when you are doing
something you know
can go south and
it might be the last thing
you will ever do.
That feeling is what
makes it unique...
Your last experience of life...
And let me let you in
on a secret about
what's going to happen
when you are gone.

Everybody moves on, eventually...

Done

Honestly, I have given up. This feeling of loneliness every morning which makes me want to never get out of my bed. Not knowing if today is when I die or just return exhausted to bed and cry myself to sleep like every other night.

I, for my age, have seen it all except love. See that's all I long for and that's all I am after. That probably is one of the reasons I could never get closer to it. The universe has a way of fucking with you when you deeply desire something.

This is where I stop pursuing you, my love, this is where I am done...

Whispers

Your whispers,

in loneliness,

drive me crazy.

Conversations that Kill You

"What if I die tomorrow?" she asked.

"My love, there is a chance you will. But let me just say this, if that happens, I will be taking the next express train that leaves the station or the next flight and jump out of it, just to be with you. Just to see you again."

"What if I die tomorrow?" I asked.

The silence killed me instantly.

False Goodbyes

The morning dew reminds me of you, the way your face glows when the light hits upon it. I see you standing right in front of me and I try to wipe it off your face with a concern that you might catch a cold.

And every time the distance is too much to cover and I just wave in the air and you wave back, sometimes thinking it's a goodbye…

Sadness

"What is it like to be able to feel everything but not being able to do anything about it?" she asked.

"It's like you are in a garden and waiting for someone to order you to breathe because they said we are low on oxygen." he answered.

"What do you mean?" she asked.

He answered with a sigh,

"It slowly kills you."

Calm

Her

Your fragrance still lingers here,
in my bed.
It's funny since
you've never been here,
but I had dreamt of you once...

What Else is Left?

I sometimes think
what could I possibly
write about love
that hasn't already
been written?

Then I think about her...

Daylight

Fallen asleep on a beach,
her head on my shoulder,
so close, yet out of reach.
Makes me feel happy,
so much that it pains,
reality makes me feel sappy.

She's still asleep, I am awake,
I wonder how much of me
this morning will take.
Her tresses long, in morning's wake,
the wind teases her,
peace is at stake.

As I notice my hand on her shoulder,
almost trying but afraid to hold her,
the sun decides to shine its light,
the wind blows, with all its might;
the transition of long walks,
foolish talks, and an unending night,
slowly fading, into the daylight.
The wind continues to tease her,
a few strands of hair, loose on her face,
I, caught up in a trance of her embrace,
fighting to keep my fingers from moving,
my hand in the air, and her eyes slowly rolling.
She opens her eyes and sees my hand,
pulls back her strands of hair,

before I have a chance.
Her head on my shoulder, she adjusts,
gets a little comfortable, a little restless,
puts her arm around mine to hold her,
says to me that I should have told her.

She points at the sunrise,
I kept looking at her and whispered:
What a sight
I opened my eyes, from another losing fight;
a dream, a clatter, so ridiculous, doesn't matter.
Made me smile, stopped me in my tracks,
on my bedside that should be empty, is her instead.

Could be a dream in a dream, I dread…

Perfection

I've heard a lot about the way universe is completely crazy about her, and then I've seen it myself.

I've seen the clouds cover the sun when she is walking down the road. I have seen the waves of the sea retreat when she stands at the shore trying to feel the cold sand under her feet.

I've seen every stranger glance back at her for a second look, for her beauty is mesmerising. I've seen the tears flowing from her eyes shine brighter than the stars that shine at night, in daylight. I've witnessed the moon make its way out of the clouds just to catch a glimpse of her at night. I've seen birds line up at her window and sing in the morning.

I've heard complete silence, not even the howl of the wind when she sleeps. I've noticed everything loves her unconditionally.

And when someone asks me why I don't tell her how I feel about her, I tell them, I can't compete with the universe. For someone so beautiful deserves more than I can give. Maybe the universe itself...

Days Like These (A Song)

An open field ends with a beach,
a shoreline, close and yet, out of reach.
A silhouette in the dark,
walks hand in hand with my shadow.

Days like these are tough,
when I want to hold her close,
as much as I wish,
she's far away, yet so close.
And I wish upon the stars
to let me hold you just once,
will it be enough,
or should I hold onto her for months?

As I start to walk on along the shore,
I see you get farther more and more,
And when I just stand still,
My body is taken over by sorrow.

Days like these are tough,
when I want to hold her close,
as much as I wish,
she's far away, yet so close.
And I wish upon the stars
to let me hold you just once,
will it be enough,
or should I hold onto her for months?

A Conversation with Her

Not too long ago, I found my self completely, utterly, stupendously, head over heels for some one. I have no idea how it happened or when it started. However, it did. And now, I am confused how to go about my everyday life. I don't really know if she knows that she's the one but when I mentioned that I caught feelings for someone and I was running away for a bit to get a grip on what's happening, she responded with "That is a big problem!" and for me that statement is a big problem.

Anyway, a couple of weeks later, I was speaking to her about this book that I was working on, and out of curiosity she asked, "What would be the name of the book?" I responded with "Petrichor." "And what's that?" she asked.

I replied, "A pleasant smell that frequently accompanies the first rain after a long period of warm, dry weather. The scent of the rain." And immediately she says, "Oh, the smell that makes it difficult for you to breathe and makes it seem like you're having an asthma attack," and starts laughing like a four-year-old. I have never been so speechless hearing someone's laughter with a spark in her eyes that made me weak in my knees. I knew then, I was completely and utterly fucked!

A Conversation
I Will Never Have with Her

"Hello! How have you been? I wanted to talk to you about something, that you may or may not already know. I don't know how or when it happened, but it did. I've liked you from a distance, but the more I got to know you and the more I talked with you, the more I was pulled towards you. It has been years since I've felt so free and myself around someone. I didn't even remember what that felt like. I understand you might have just been polite, listening to me when you did, and I, who does not usually open up in front of anyone, surprised myself, when I shared all that, I did with you. I laughed at myself after that, however. This has never happened to me before.

Since the first day we started speaking, you felt like a friend who I haven't met for a long time. You're strong, confident, funny and smart and an amazingly caring and warm person with a devilish personality that makes me want to sit with you hours on end and explore more of your thoughts. But I always pull myself back as I don't want to lose what I have. The more time I spent with you, the more I realized that I am drowning deeper and deeper, not just in conversations with you but in your eyes.

Every time I spoke with you, I felt warm and felt at home. And I cannot explain how that is possible and I haven't experienced this before. You know my story and you know the demons I've fought to be standing here today. The more time I spent with you, the more I realized that I just don't want to be someone on the outside looking in.

And I understand that my feelings towards you won't be reciprocated and that's ok. I don't want to miss a chance, if there is any, to be together; as the thought of us being together keeps me up at night, excited. What you want to decide with the feelings that I just shared with you, will completely and solely be your decision."

I have this whole conversation in my head that I want to have with her, but I don't want to lose her at the same time… I've always been a master at hiding how I feel or so I thought, cause only when I am with her, is when I don't have to force a smile on my face. And when the realization creeped in, that all this can just vanish with one single conversation, it makes me want to stop breathing. So, I decided to not have this conversation and keep things the way they are.

I have been missing home for a long time, and I want to feel being at home for just a little longer.

A Conversation
I Want to have with Her

"You walk into your own torments, with head held high, no idea what the outcome will be, no idea where this road will take you, no one to trust and rely on in need. How do you manage to get all this done?" I asked her in the midst of an extended conversation we weren't supposed to have.

She replied "I walk with my head high because everyone else is expecting me to look down. No one knows the outcome; we are only here for the journey which I intend to enjoy. No one needs trust if you know that you are enough for yourself and confident enough to face your problems head on." After a small pause, she continued, "I hold a knife every night to my wrist and tell myself that I am stronger than this, I could cut myself but I don't and that's how I get all this done."

After a moment of silence, I knew she was like me and all I could say was, "Yes, I know the feeling."

Cold Water

A sprinkle here and a sprinkle there,
sometimes too hard to bear,
winter nights are all I dread,
and sometimes I don't really care.

As the hours of dawn approach,
the memories of past encroach,
what did we find, what we lost,
as the rain turns to frost.

I never did realise,
the things we did surmise,
winter mornings and cold water,
that's what my heart is after.
It doesn't really matter now.
I sometimes breathe and
sometimes forget,
after she left me stranded here,
there's nothing more in life to regret.

I fight the urge to get through the night,
no more will left to survive,
maybe what's done is done, so long,
I am living to just die.

I never did realise,
the things we did surmise,
winter mornings and cold water,
that's what my heart is after.
It doesn't really matter now.
I sometimes breathe and
sometimes forget,
after she left me stranded here,
there's nothing more in life to regret.

Always on My Mind

This one's not about love or loss, or the essence of it all. This one's about life. And what that is, is a mystery in its own. There are things that I need to do, that are always on my mind. I do them, and I don't really remember throughout the day if, in fact, I have done them. These things, they take up space in my head, give me migraines that are beyond expression on paper.

I have to remember to sleep and then make sure to wake up in the morning. I sometimes don't want to, but morning waits for no one and it just arrives. So, I end up not sleeping all night to make sure I am awake when the morning arrives. I have to. Get up. Show up. Smile. Survive. Repeat.

Watch the road when I cross it. Call it suicidal tendencies acting up, sometimes, I don't wait for the car to pass. If I am at a crossing, I'd jump headfirst in front because I don't have the patience to let someone pass before me, because I am behind and I need to get where I am going. Need to remind myself to wait.

I forget to breathe sometimes when your thought comes to mind. Nothing hurts like the image of your smiling face and the realization that I'll never touch that smile or make you laugh. Fuck! I made it about love again, didn't I? But, if not love or loss, what the fuck are we living for? What are we looking forward to everyday? Who do you get out of bed for every morning? Love is constant or the loss of it. That's always on my mind.

And if I remember that love exists or the lack of it in my life, I think I'll make it...

September Love

I've been stopping myself from falling for her over and over. I want to run my fingers on her neck and whisper in her ears, with kisses on her shoulders, undressing her to the depths of her soul. I don't want our lips to meet just yet, for when they do, I want it to be magic.

I want to touch those sea-salt lips, hold her face in between my palms, before I finally give in to love...

I want to trace constellations on the curves of her body. I want you to call me home and be my home for me.

I want us to live and love gracefully. I know my imagination gets the best of me sometimes, but I want this in reality...

Falling

I read this Rudy Francisco quote which goes:

"I write best when I am either falling in love or falling apart."

I do the same and right now, I'm falling in love with someone, and falling apart at the same time because I fell for someone with whom there's no possibility of being together...

So, some days I write about love and most days, about how painful love can be...

Trip & Fall

As I run away from these feelings again, from tripping and falling ridiculously in love. I remember how every time love took a piece of my soul and left me with nothing but an empty shell, hurt and pain and for some reason yearning for more of it...

Finding Her

I write of the moon, and the waves falling on the shores and the sound they make. I write the way she ties her hair in four steps.

I know people look for a meaning in what I write, they try to find her even, but I keep her hidden in well created metaphors. A tornado. I, the wave; her, the shore. Her laughter wrapped in innocence, her tresses, shade for the beloved.

I can go on and on about how she is present in every word of my poetry, like a well-placed comma. Our conversations on the lines of fiction and reality, blurry, like my vision gets when I spend a little too much time around her, knowing well saying anything about how I feel could ruin everything that I have.

So, I don't, and cherish what is, and try not to regret what could never be.

But it's hard to deal with the what ifs that follow in a poet's mind...

Not Going to Happen

Not going to happen,
I keep saying this to
myself when I look at her.
As I write this,
I'm running away from her,
from the feelings
that I have for her.
I don't know if she's
the right person,
at a very wrong time
or she's here to show
that I, even after all the
damage, can still love.
Like before and even more.
I've read somewhere,
that each love takes extra
strength and hurts deeper
than the previous ones.
And I have a feeling, this
one's going to
rip me open like
never before.

A Broken Mind

I am pacing in my room, lights off, a weak humidifier in the corner with her faint smell…

I Imagine: I am lying on the bed, my head pressed against her chest. I can hear her heartbeat, in sync with mine. Each breath like a wave rising and falling, her heartbeat a lullaby slowly caressing me to sleep.

Reality: I'm still pacing in my room, lights off. I lie down on the bed, my head pressed against a hard pillow which gives me a headache every morning. All I hear is silence amidst the dark, afraid, of the monster lurking, who might consume me if I open my eyes… I can't sleep with this thought in my head.

I Imagine: She's standing in the dark, bedside, with her arm out, as if to say, I'm here and you're safe…

Reality: I don't open my eyes, I lie in pain, until my alarm goes off…

Misfits

We, the artists, are the misfits of the world.

We write our pain,
the crumbling thoughts
that gives us anxiety
on a cold winter night,
the monsters we slay in the dark,
the pricking pain in our hearts.
We pick locks with our words,
to make the pain flow
which the heart holds.
We paint pictures with our words,
we pour out our love
and call it fiction.

We're sometimes too afraid,
to say what we want to say,
because we don't want to be
called crazy.

And sometimes we get high
and post deep dark
secrets of our minds,
and when we're sober,
we realise we need to
cut down on alcohol…

We sing, we dance,

we're always in a trance,
we love hard and lose harder,
unwary of the fall.

We write songs about romance,
we kill in our novels,
the characters we hate in real life.
and create a perfect crime.

Let the misfits be a part of your life,
Sharing a morning tea
or a couple of coffees.
Don't ever let your heart bleed,
tell a misfit of what your heart feels,
And let them create art from it.

The Traveller

"I travel from time to time and fall in love with total strangers hopelessly. It sort of breaks my heart that we can never be together and that gives me the satisfaction that I can still feel something."

Improvised

There is this emptiness, this void I am trying to fill with your memories. I am afraid, as I am running short of memories of you. I remember every time we spoke, shook hands or looked at each other with a smile and then we avoided each other without remorse. I remember how we met the first time and the events that followed that day. I remember all the details.

I have filled this void as much as I could but it's still half empty. My only option now is to fill it with the memories I have of our future together from my dreams. I have looked far too deep into the future, a future with you. Where you are always by my side and there's no losing you.

At this point I have improvised a love tale that does not exist, but one which keeps me hoping for a happy ending, eventually. At this point, you have become my muse…

Warm You Up

All I want is
to be the blanket
that you pull up
to wrap yourself in,
in the middle
of the night,
when a cool breeze
wakes you up
during winter.

Angels

She feels a little broken every time something doesn't go as planned. She has her own way of getting things done. She kicks off those heels and sits in a corner, head down and in complete silence.

The only way you will ever get to talk to her is on her terms. She is a child at heart, with a smile that will remind you of someone you always miss. She is an open book, but encrypted. The only way to decrypt her is to trust her and hope that she trusts you too. Then, you'll get to read all the broken promises, tales of tough times and bad decisions engraved on her skin.

She is as beautiful as it gets, with as many complications you would expect from someone who looks like that and there's no one like her. They wouldn't call anyone an *angel* if they didn't think they have the power to rule everyone's heart, be what it may be, sorrow or happiness –

Angels are beautiful…

Black & White

This is not the way
I had planned my life…
Looking out of foggy windows
with incomplete thoughts
in black and white…

See

Can you see?
There, in the distance
where there are
no clouds and
sunlight kisses the
earth…

that's where,
I wait for your
return…

Surviving You

The farther I went,
the closer you came,
the closer I tried to come,
the farther you stepped away...
Is there something that I don't see here?
Is there something that I am missing?
Are we still the same souls intertwined,
long ago, due to the sheer
need of survival.
Now that the apocalypse has ended and we
have survived,
can we stop playing this game of hide and
seek and just be who we are?
I, the one lost in the ocean of your
eyes, drowned, gasping for breath, trying
to stay afloat.
You, the tsunami trying to drown me every
time you close your
eyes and stop your tears.
I could surely survive another
apocalypse,
but tell me, how do I survive you?

Tale of the Red Scarf

They don't say much, they have been together for far too long and understand each other just by a glance. She loves him for what he was, is and will become. She decided that when she said 'yes' to spend her life with him.

Sometimes, she thinks it's all over. The love, the romance, the 2 a.m. calls, all of it. It just stopped. He understands, things have changed. He thinks what they need is love, but it's lost.

All it took for him to find it again was a breeze that took her red scarf along with it and the way he ran after it, to catch it before it kissed the ground. It made her realize that nothing has changed; it's him, the one she loved.

He comes back with the scarf, gently kisses her forehead, hugs her, and says, "I'm sorry." She whispers back in his ear, "I know." The scarf always saved them, after all that's how they met the first time.

Knowing

It's 3:45 a.m. as I start to write this note for you, knowing you may not read this. Knowing even if you read this, you may not acknowledge this. Knowing even if you did acknowledge, I will never know and it will not matter anyway.

I know deep down that I love you with all I have, with all I am, in my own mysterious silence and weirdness. I know you don't love me back and I am ok with the fact that you may never. Sometimes, knowing too much can be dangerous. And, for the past few months, you are all I know and it's killing me...

November

It's November and it's starting to get cold. The days don't bother me much. However, the nights have a different story.

I haven't been sleeping well and when I do, I hear a voice. Your voice, calling me into the unknown and I follow it without thinking twice, hoping to catch a glimpse of you because I've been dreaming about you too much lately, daydreaming...

The other day I followed someone, thinking that it was you. I miss you terribly and it's November and it's too cold for me to stand outside and pass out without memories...

I am starting to black out now because of the cold. So, I won't know if you showed up at my door, I need to know, if you feel the cold too...

Did you come?

Listen

Close your eyes,
let it all in,
listen,
just listen,
the whistling of the wind,
let the wilderness
speak to you in its way.

Let it all unfold,
now,
let it all go,
scream your lungs out.

Now,
How do you feel?
Let that sink in...

What She Said

"It's too late now, we can't be together anymore," I said, in a shaky voice.

In a calm voice, she replied,

"It's never too late if it feels right."

Maybe – The Beginning

Maybe, what we need is a silver lining. A line which distinguishes between the blood-soaked sun and the ocean when it drowns in it every day, only to come up again the next.

Maybe, all we need is another tomorrow, where we accept our flaws, apologise for our mistakes, love without being scared and live life carefree.

Maybe, then, we could have another chance.

Maybe Part – 1

She roams around with those saggy bags underneath her eyes and all I can think of is, what could keep someone as beautiful as her awake all night?

Then I look at myself in the mirror and notice the bags under my eyes and find my answer.

Love…

I love her and she loves someone else. I knew I didn't have a chance, but someone who didn't even care to notice her doesn't deserve her. She deserves better…

Maybe me…

Maybe…

Maybe Part – 2

And then sometimes 'I' isn't an answer, 'we' or 'us' sounds much better in comparison. All I think of is maybe tomorrow I will be noticed, sipping coffee from an empty cup, sitting right across her as always, unnoticed as if I don't exist.

Moments like these, I question myself if I really am flesh and blood; if I really do exist. And then like every other night, I pick up the knife from the side-table, kept beside the sleeping pills and hold it to my skin till I feel the sharp pain in my soul...

I keep it away, consoling myself maybe tomorrow she will notice. Maybe tomorrow she will call my name.

Maybe...

Maybe Part – 3

He sits right across her, sipping coffee from an empty cup every day. She notices him trying to muster up the courage and talk to her. She hopes maybe today is the day that he might finally approach and say how he feels about her.

She doesn't give him a clue and hopes he would still understand. She knew for quite some time that the statement "head over heels" is an understatement for how he felt about her. They both loved each other in their own understanding of what love is.

Him, too afraid to face a denial and her, hurt too many times to open up to someone new. They may or may not be together if they take a chance. But they won't take that chance. They can just hope for the other to approach and imagine how different things would have been. Only if they did.

She sits on her bed at night, sleepless, writing in her diary how much she loved him, that person across the table that drinks coffee from an empty cup, just to see her. She had his number and every night she typed in a message "Coffee tomorrow? Maybe a filled cup?" but never had the courage to send it across. This time fate had played its part and she hit send, instead of deleting. She waited all night long hoping for a reply from him with a "Yes!" but received nothing. Maybe it was all in her head. Maybe he has given up on me, she thought. Maybe it was too late.

He never decided how he would respond when she eventually did reach out. He didn't have a clue what to reply...

He doesn't. Maybe he would just show up, she thought.

Maybe...

Maybe – The Final Chapter

The next day, he showed up shivering, wearing a red tie hoping she hadn't forgotten. To his surprise, she was already waiting, wearing a red dress. He waved from a distance with a smile on his face, seeing a reaction which would make your dampened heart glow with a smile. A smile on her face, looking at you. He never had that response before when anyone saw him. It was what he had wished all along and that was what he had received.

She was never so happy to see someone, as she did when he showed up. The fear of being stood up does that to you. Finally, someone showed up and she hoped he continues to do so. He knew in his heart he would. They sat together for an hour, with her sharing stories of all the times she caught him looking at her. Him, being as clueless as he could be, didn't know what to say. He just kept his head down, as shy as a baby scared of looking at her. Then she asked, "Are you not going to say anything?" He replied, "My questions have been answered." "How so?" she asked. "I always wondered, maybe, if you ever noticed me and you always did."

"My 'maybe' was always a reality not just yours," she said.

"Ours."

"Maybe we are meant to be."

Correction: he said, there's no "maybe", We Are.

Closing Arguments

Whenever we have an argument, the only thing that seems sensible to be done is kiss you.

Kiss you on your mouth because I could never muster up the courage to tell you to shut up.

And that's the politest way I can think of to say 'I am sorry'...

When Night Comes On

He held her hand and pulled her closer. Close enough that the only distance between them was a sign of respect that waited for her approval to eliminate it.

She asked him, "What will happen if I give in now?"

"What do you think?" he asked.

"You will leave me once you have my body as everyone else did. Everyone else before you disappeared in the morning," she replied.

With a smile on his face, he said in her ear, "Then don't give in, stay with me just like this till it feels right. And if you doubt that I will leave, hold me tight until I bleed. I promise you; I will be here as long as you need me to be. I am in this for life, and not here for your body. I intend to touch your soul."

I asked her, "Will you be in my arms in the morning?" She had fallen asleep by then.

I woke up in the morning to an empty bed with no sign of her.

Another cruel dream, taking away my sanity piece by piece.

I should have known better; the ways universe keeps playing with my head and a mind that fucking remembers every dream as if it were a reality...

Silence

Silence had its own interpretation of love. I loved her silently and she thought I had no interest in her.

It's a funny thing, this silence.

2 AM

There's something about 2 a.m., the silent voices start to shout in my ears. The body is tired from all the things that took place during the day, yet the soul is wide awake, restless for reasons I am not certain of.

I am sitting alone at my desk trying to describe your picture in words. Sometimes I feel your presence right beside me, guiding me, like this is how you want the world to see you. Your fragrance startles me when I doze off looking at your picture, as if keeping me awake to finish what I had started.

You, my love, have left me years ago, yet here you are with me every step of the way. I believe you are guiding me towards you but somewhere in my heart and mind I feel I'm just headed towards my destruction.

Well, it's 2 a.m. and I am lonely like every other night, clinging onto the phone hoping you will reach out. I know you are going to read this and just smile and say 'I won't'. And I will sleep with the thought, maybe you will...

That's what you do at this time of night. You hope...

Strings

There are strings in the deepest corners of my brain that connects with my nerves in my head. They hold every memory in time I had with you like chapters in a book, read and closed and never reached for again. There are your pictures hanging from these strings which I keep visiting, just to remember your face.

Every string holds a memory, a picture or a letter which I held dear from our meetings but never sent them to you, fearing you may just discard them. Then there are those strings where there is uncertainty, they are just jumbled up in the clumsiest way.

They are my dreams; dreams I saw with you. A future which seems improbable currently, considering the paths we are on. Beyond all this, there is a door, yes, a door in my mind.

I can't let you in just yet. You must first untangle the strings of my mind to get there...

Love

They tell me, you don't love me. You never loved me.

I tell them they are mistaken.

"She has always loved me and she will always love me. You only let go of someone you love the most."

The Final Dialogue

"Am I supposed to feel the way I do when I look in the mirror?" she asked him.

"How do you mean?" he asked.

"Like something used and then discarded every single time after I have served the purpose of men who had no intention of keeping their promises.

"Like a life vest they wear to keep themselves alive but don't realise that they suck all the air from it killing it in the process.

"Like a thread which cuts through your skin and hurts like nothing ever did. You understand what I mean, right?"

He slowly came closer and said, "I understand how you feel. I can relate."

"How so?" she asked.

"It's the same as you love someone, and they don't see you and you have to see them going through all this pain only too late to understand that someone loved you all along."

He didn't realise what he had just said.

"Is it too late now?" she asked.

"It's never too late in love." he replied.

Thirty-Five

I am surprised I made it this far in life. From what I remember my exit from this world could have been on 12th October 2002. It's been 20 years and I write this on 12th October 2022. It's about the same time I met that dreaded accident. It's a bit premature but I think if I made it this far, I'll make it another month to see thirty-five.

Thirty-five and I still can't believe it. Thirty-five years of highs and lows, couple of thousand cigarettes smoked. Loved hard and crashed low. Unrequited love stories, painful long nights, never been to a bar, so I missed all the bar fights, let the hurt hurt, so it could hurt less. Keep falling in love, and become numb, to love less. Cry my heart out, spend the night out, smoking cigars while breaking up fights and telling people to chill the fuck out. Walk home from work to an empty room, where no one waits, learn to be alone and make peace with death. I have done it all, yet I still fall.

I fall short on responsibilities, cause when I was carrying them out, it pissed people off. They took away my son, left me broken, made me hit rock bottom. Because they thought I would appreciate them. Well, guess what, here I am, with all the scars, and wounds healed and unhealed, walking with conviction, no tears, fake smiles, scared, scary, a little weary, soft, yet so hard, I don't let anyone in anymore. You can knock, you try and leave the door. You were in my space and you'll never be this close. I have changed and I am glad that I didn't before. You saw who I was and now you'll see what

I've become. I've read somewhere you don't mature with age, but with damage. Look at the carnage that they made, left me to just fade away, like I didn't matter. Away, like I was a lost cause; away, yet I still don't know who gave them the fucking permission to throw me out of the house. Away, but I know something, I'll come back, because all I have is my fucking mind, it's dark sometimes but they've never seen the way it shines and I will make my way back, my own way…

I still love the same way I did. Even harder and deeper. I look for meaningful conversations now, I am no longer attracted to outer beauty, that'll eventually fade. That's what they taught me. I've learnt love is not a feeling, loving someone is a decision you both make. I avoid drama, I know now I must let go of love sometimes. But I make it known that I love them, because I've read somewhere that true love will stay. Thirty-five years and still looking for love with all the damage and bandages around the heart, knees and elbows scraped from falling too hard, no one to notice or catch my heart, sometimes noticed and left to suffer alone. Unrequited love stories and so much fun, conversations in my head that never took place, fiction is a work of art and being in love is sometimes a cruel place. So, I hide it, fight it, sometimes unapologetically brush it under the bed, with eyes red, sleepless, careless, I couldn't care less. Write with conviction, with annotation, a love letter, old school, everyone calls me a fool as if they weren't in love once in their lives, sever the ties, some people say, you must be precise. I don't listen to them anyway.

In the past thirty-five years, one thing I figured out about love is this: no matter how old you are, you will find love at every stage of your life. Sometimes they are a lesson. Sometimes they are the real deal, but the timing isn't right. The more heartbreak you've endured, the deeper you fall in love every time. No matter how much you want to stay in the shallow end of the pool, the ocean will pull you in eventually. Let it, I say dive in headfirst and surprise it. Sometimes confession is not an option, when you have too much to lose, you choose what you want to keep and devise a strategy to use. You'll eventually find someone who stays or someone who will come back or you'll meet someone from your past again. But the past is not an option, unless you never confessed.

I know I still talk about self-harm sometimes, but believe me, I'm trying. When I write, I write about how lonely it gets, but that's not the problem. I have grown comfortable with my company, in sync with nature and its harmony. It's when they fuck my peace and want a piece of soul, that's when it gets dark and thoughts take shape in the crevices of my brain. I write about them to not act on them. I can't talk about them, as no one would understand. How it feels, to look into the mirror and see yourself broken, how some people call me a masterpiece and have no idea, how much time it took for me to piece myself together to get out of bed that morning. Thirty-five years of brokenness doesn't disappear with a few months of doing something marvellous. They say I am worthy and their actions says otherwise. They ask me to be happy and tell me to stay away from people who make me smile. It's a fucking shit show out here. Rules and regulations to adhere.

At thirty-five, a father, a fighter, a lover, and a writer. A poet for the beloved, a lonesome man for the masses, head over heels in love, navigating through a crisis. Some things in life never change. Experiences mould, I know my limits now, I know when to fold…

Petrichor

The loud screams of the clouds, during a thunderstorm. The pitter patter of rain and the soothing calmness that follows. The sun, slowly peeking through the clouds, and everything starts to smile as its rays touches the earth, like a lover caressing the tresses of a beloved, holding her, loving her.

Every raindrop that fell, shines its brightest. The puddles of water, a loud chatter, parks filled with people after everything turned gloomy and dark and turned bright and oh so much light, tying their shoelaces, leaving traces in everything touched by the smile on their faces. Deep breaths to smell the earth, young and adults, finding their places. The smell of petrichor, the scent of the earth, makes you forget in that moment, the battles you're fighting, the closing death bed, a life lived recklessly and how much of a wreck you are and how you cannot care less…

Holding hands of the one you love, comparing them to the sun that shines, the rain drops that make you wet, sometimes they make you cry. Hold on to this feeling now, hold on your gaze in those bright sparkling eyes, for she'll be beside you till the end of times. When your world comes crashing down, remember how the earth survives a thunderstorm. You fill your hearts with all you see and sometimes you don't see clearly. Sometimes it gets hard to breathe when you're out in the calm.

It's not always rainbows and sunshine, when children cry and toddlers whine, you leave them for a speck of time and they're never the same. They fall on their faces flat, laugh out loud, louder they cry and everything is different.

And as I sit here all by myself, watching them trip and laugh and roll, the kids, the adults and the one I love. I catch a glimpse of her again. Walking around, hand in hand with someone she loves and who loves her back. A smile on her face and a close embrace. I see myself fall from grace, like every other time. Tears roll down my face, our eyes meet and I respond with grace, a cigarette in one hand and a bottle of coke, I say cheers and gulp it all in a go.

As pain makes its way again, I smell the petrichor, healing my soul. I sit here in nothingness, losing everything I never owned. The mind has played its tricks, I am more in love than ever. If tomorrow is my end, I've lived promises of forever. And if I had just one more chance, I'd tell her how much I love her…

About the Author

Mohammed Abrar Ahmed is the author behind @thficklepoet. He is a poet and the author of the new poetry collection Petrichor.

His previous works include: The Years Gone By and Daydreams and Midnight Realities.

With over a decade of writing and sharing on his social media platforms like Facebook, Instagram etc., Abrar navigates through loss, pain and letting go, in his newest collection of poetry and short stories.

Abrar has traveled extensively around South East Asia, and sometimes represents stories learnt and experienced during his journey through his characters.

Abrar currently resides in Ruwais, UAE and is working on his novel. He looks forward to where the next chapter will take him.

https://linktr.ee/theficklepoet

www.ingramcontent.com/pod-product-compliance
Lightning Source LLC
Chambersburg PA
CBHW070432010526
44118CB00014B/2015